The Execution of Saddam Hussein: An American-Iranian Game

Thank you for every thing Dr Turner

Mohamed F. Siddig

The Execution of Saddam Hussein: An American-Iranian Game

Mohamed Fadl Ali

iUniverse, Inc.
New York Lincoln Shanghai

The Execution of Saddam Hussein: An American-Iranian Game

iUniverse books may be ordered through booksellers or by contacting:

iUniverse
2021 Pine Lake Road, Suite 100
Lincoln, NE 68512
www.iuniverse.com
1-800-Authors (1-800-288-4677)

Translated by Babiker Abbas
Edited by Marcia Craig

ISBN: 978-0-595-43649-1 (pbk)
ISBN: 978-0-595-87976-2 (ebk)

Printed in the United States of America

The original manuscript of this book was written in Arabic; some expressions may be unfamiliar to the English reader.

We can easily forgive a child who is afraid of dark, the real tragedy of life is when men are afraid of light.—Plato

From the Author

To whosoever opposes and resists the destructive international outburst led by the current American administration under the neoconservatives; to whosoever opposes terror and its retaliatory terror, states' terror, and organizations' terror; I present this humble effort.

Keywords: trial of Saddam Hussein; American invasion of Iraq; Iranian hegemony; Middle East; nuclear threat of Iran; Saddam Hussein's regime

Contents

Foreword

I came to know the author during the mid-1990s in Cairo. By that time he was very concerned about the Sudanese cause. I realized that he had been writing about the Sudanese question since the beginning of the 1990s, opposing the regime of the National Islamic Front in his country. His position had extended to a schism with anything related to the Islamists. Even though I did not agree with most of his perceptions, as they were semi-absolute with regard to this issue, I testify to his deep vision. I remember in his book *The False Caliphate* published in Egypt in 1997, the author issued a famous caution—a warning to the West about using the Islamists as a bargaining chip against Arab regimes. He mentioned that such pressure would backfire on the West, particularly on the United States of America. The author chastised Muslim and Arab countries for their inability to deal with religious fanaticism. He accused them of turning their backs on the Sudanese people. He alleged that the Sudanese people had been subjected to horror and gross violations of rights by the Islamists, amid silence and sometimes support of some Arab regimes and Islamist groups.

Fadl Ali talked bitterly and sharply about Arab Islamists and their role in Sudan during the first years of the Islamic government in the 1990s. *The False Caliphate* was a warning bell about the danger of al-Qaeda and the Islamists. I remember my conversation with the Sudanese writer, his keen political analysis, and his injunctions about the dangers of Iran with respect to Iraq. This was a long time before the American invasion of Iraq. It is evident that Mohamed Fadl Ali was among the first writers to anticipate the perils engendered by Iranian hegemony over and control of Iraq.

These hazards have been exposed as the American war on Iraq has progressed. The fumbling of the American administration has made it apparent that it was not prepared for this undertaking. The American invasion of Iraq, followed by a mysterious deal whereby Iraq was offered as a free gift to the extremist Iranian government, is one of the most glaring political and strategic mistakes of the twenty-first century. Fadl Ali predicted all of this through many famous and documented articles and discussions. The author was among the first to address the first anti-war gathering in Canada. He is known for his activity among groups that oppose the American war on Iraq through demonstrations in various forums such as libraries and street gatherings.

It is evident that Mohamed Fadl Ali is a farseeing author. His ability to analyze and foresee the future has surpassed other well known Arab writers who supported the war on Iraq, and for whom the situation in Iraq nullified all expectations. Fadl Ali has also seen farther than a considerable number of famous American journalists from the Bush administration and the American neoconservative sector, whose writings on the Iraqi question found the same ill fate.

I read most of the *The Execution of Saddam Hussein: An American-Iranian Game* and I feel that the author has produced a thorough analysis of the current state of affairs in Iraq. He has dared to inform us about the secret Iranian state in Iraq, in addition to detailing the Iranian hegemony over the new Iraqi state under American occupation. Every passing day adds credentials to what Fadl Ali has written regarding Iranian domination and control of Iraq and the consequences of directing the religious and sectarian court that tries the former Iraqi president, Saddam Hussein.

Regarding solutions to the Iraqi dilemma, Fadl Ali seeks to avoid the spread of anarchy to the rest of the region or a conflict that will encourage Iranian expansion. He is particularly prescient in discussing the trial of the former Iraqi dictator, Saddam Hussein, a former American ally who was abandoned by the Americans and left to deal with his historical enemies alone. The author presents an intelligent analysis, worthy of attention from those tied by strategic and security affairs to current events in Iraq.

Mohamed Nasser al-Jobouri

An Iraqi Writer

Canada

November 1, 2005

Prologue

Most of the information contained in this book was addressed by the author through articles published between 2003 and 2006 in the newspaper and on the Internet. The book analyzes events of the American invasion of Iraq—the invasion which turned into Iranian occupation of Iraq. The book focuses on the trial of the former Iraqi president Saddam Hussein. This trial was an important Iranian project in Iraq but was actually accomplished by the American president G. W. Bush. The American invasion of Iraq turned into a victory for Iran without loss of Iranian money or blood. The American president unintentionally extended Iranian territory in the Middle-East.

1

The American Iraq, Hell Speaks

Iraq is the cradle of several ancient civilizations. It has been, through its long history, an attraction point for invaders. All foreign invading campaigns against Iraq were characterized by utter barbarism and violence. Most of these invasions were justified by divine reasons. However, the common denominator of all these ancient as well as recent invaders has been the targeting of cultural values and symbols of Iraq. In this regard, there is no difference between the invasion by the Mongols, who burned libraries and science houses and killed people mercilessly, and the recent American invasion; the Americans also destroyed historical monuments, and killed and tortured Iraqi citizens.

Moreover, the American invasion has kept Iraq under the mercy of barbaric militias that are affiliated with religious political parties. These parties are in league with the Islamic Republic of Iran, which rules Iraq today. These Iraqi Iranian militias commit crimes under the protection of and in collaboration with American forces. Young American soldiers who are ignorant of the theater in which they practice killing and torture are not to blame in this war. Blame should be directed to the American political leadership which planned and executed the illegitimate invasion of Iraq that has resulted in so many atrocities.

One of the consequences of this invasion is the clandestine pro-Iran militia; some of them operate covertly under the guise of the army and the police. These militias embrace terrorist policies after the Iranian model, such as restricting women's freedom in the streets and persecuting non-Muslims. These activities have led the Christian minority to call for international protection. Such practices were not in vogue during Saddam Hussein's regime. One of the heinous crimes committed by these pro-Iran militias was destruction of the statue of the founder of the historic city of Baghdad. This kind of desecration was inflicted by the Taliban government when it destroyed the Buddha statue and other temples in Afghanistan. In this book the reader will find details of incidents involving

Christian sects terrorized by pro-Iran Iraqi Shiite militias that rule Iraq under protection of the American army.

Before delving into the details of little-known realities about occupied Iraq and the trial of Saddam Hussein, I want to draw attention to an aspect that is unknown to most of the American people, to the truth of what has been taking place in Iraq in their name. In the aftermath of the fall of Baghdad, the Bush administration performed the greatest fraud in recent history—he deliberately concealed important facts about the invasion and its immediate consequences. A brief background of the history of Iraq and the ancient Muslim world is offered to cast light on a religious crisis that took place more than 14 centuries ago that has a direct impact on the current situation.

This historical religious crisis resulted in a schism in the Muslim world. The schism opened at the time when the prophet Mohamed (peace be upon him) died. It was a religious, sectarian, and political schism triggered by the controversy of who would assume the caliphate after Mohamed's death. The Shiites, a minority of the Muslim populace, were of the view that the caliphate should be held by a descendant of Mohamed. The bulk of the Muslims held that there were factors other than blood relations to the prophet that should determine who would lead the Muslims. This bulk group, about 85 percent of the Muslim populace, came to be called Sunni and their viewpoint prevailed. The Sunnis chose Abu Bakar al-Siddiq, Mohamed's close friend and the first to believe in his message. In order to lead Islam, Abu Bakar sacrificed his wealth, his social status, and endured persecution and hardship. Like other first believers of Islam, Abu Bakar suffered discrimination and torture perpetrated by idol worshipers, and had to flee his birthplace city, Mecca, in the Arab peninsula now called Saudi Arabia.

The political conflict that ensued after the death of the prophet Mohamed aggravated the differences between Sunni and Shiite. As time passed, each sect developed distinct beliefs, evolving its own school of thought, prayer, and interpretation of the holy Quran. The differences between Sunni and Shiite perspectives became so extensive that it became impossible to reach a common ground. Sunni Muslims populate five continents with a high concentration in the Middle East, the Indian subcontinent, Africa, and other countries in Asia. Shiites, who represent 15 percent of Muslims, are found in the Middle East, some places in Asia, and the Indian subcontinent. Shiites are concentrated in Iran, where they have political and military leadership and in Iraq, where they have holy sites. The deep schism between Sunnis and Shiites—views on religious issues, interpretations of the *sharia,* and in their ways of thinking—was stagnant for several centuries.

This schism appeared again and deepened after the Iranian Islamic revolution of 1979 led by Ayat Allah al-Khomeini who transformed Iran from a civil state into a fanatic theocratic state. Since its inception, the Islamic Republic of Iran has had a hostile attitude toward the entire world, including other Muslims. During the revolution, Khomeini condoned heavy bloodshed and violation of the rights of Iranian people, particularly non-Muslim minorities. Many non-Muslims fled Iran. The aggressive attitude of the new Islamic Iranian regime extended to foreign embassies culminating in the famous hostage-taking at the American embassy in 1979. According to some sources, Mahmoud Ahmadinejad, the current Iranian president, was one of the planners of this incident. From what we have seen of his presidency, his personality fits such a role. He is an aggressive person that embodies the malicious principles of Khomeini.

At the time when Iraq was under Saddam's rule, most of the Iraqi Shiites sympathized with the new revolution in Iran. The Iraqi Shiites, most of whom were naïve, revered Khomeini. They saw holiness in him that made his personality a miracle and gave him extraordinary powers. The intellectuals of the Iraqi Shiites had organized themselves in religious political parties a long time ago. However, Saddam Hussein adopted repressive policies against the religious parties——Sunni and Shiite—and they were motivated to flee the country. The Iraqi Shiite political parties found an example in Khomeini's revolution. The leadership and cadres of the *Da'wa* party and the Supreme Council of the Islamic Revolution started moving to Iran, organizing themselves in camps there. In these camps, they received military training in explosive devices and assassination. Later, they were given the necessary resources and sent to destabilize the socialist, secular Iraq and transform it into a fanatic religious state after the Iranian example. Even though they failed in this endeavor for three decades of Saddam's rule, they succeeded with George W. Bush's help in 2003. By removing Saddam Hussein, the Bush administration shuffled the security cards of the Middle East and the gulf region, a deed unprecedented in the international relations of modern history. The Shiite political parties who rule Iraq after Saddam Hussein, including Ibrahim al-Jaa'fari, are linked to Iran to the extent that they cannot be separated from the Iranian leadership that endangers international peace and security.

When Khomeini called for exporting his Islamic revolution to the entire Muslim world, Iraq was the first target because of its Shiite population. The then American president Jimmy Carter and all Sunni Muslim and Arab countries, particularly the oil-rich gulf sheikhdoms, supported Saddam Hussein. Those countries stood firm to deter the Iranian strategy of expansion and exportation of the bloody, dark Islamic revolution to other regions, particularly to Iraq. By 1980,

Saddam's intelligence officers, after discovering a plan to blow-up some strategic services, began arresting followers of Iraqi religious political parties that sympathized with Iran. This coincided with the renewal of an old border dispute between Iraq and Iran which increased tension between the two countries.

The Iran-Iraq war erupted in 1980 and continued for eight years. In this war several million were killed and the economies of Iraq, Iran, and the gulf sheikhdoms suffered. During this long war, Sunni Muslim countries and the West supported Saddam and he managed to withstand it. Khomeini believed that he could impose a new expansionist strategy by defeating Iraq. Ironically, after the international community offered cooperation and sacrifice to deter the Iranian expansionist policy in the twentieth century, George W. Bush, by supporting Iraqi religious parties related to Iran, allowed Khomeini to realize his ambitions in the twenty-first century. By invading Iraq, Bush helped to establish a clandestine secret Iranian presence in Iraq that controls the political, economic, and military apparatus of the Iraqi state. It is bizarre that this costly war has been financed by the American taxpayer. The money spent in this war would be sufficient to solve many world crises and would be better spent on alleviating poverty and diseases such as AIDS. A huge amount of American blood has been shed in a war that has nothing to do with American security and national interests. On the contrary, the American national interests are now under the shadow of the growing terror which has resulted from American transgressions on Iraqi soil.

This historical background is an attempt to shed light on the ancient sectarian rivalry between Shiites and Sunnis. This ancient schism deepened with Khomeini's revolution after the Iran-Iraq war. Since the Iran-Iraq war, Iran has tried to inflict revenge against the Muslim countries that supported Saddam Hussein. It has been shown that the invasion of Iraq was supported by faked intelligence. At the head of the security strategists that duped American espionage was Ahmed al-Jalabi, a man also accused of stealing millions of dollars from a Jordanian bank. Al-Jalabi was a leader of deceptive intelligence cells and executed what had been dictated to him by Iran. In a rare precedent in international conflict, Iran was able to drag her historical foes, the United States and Sunni Iraqis, who had deprived Iran from exporting the Islamic revolution, into this war. Iran planned this conflict and now, like a hero of an Oriental saga, she watches her foes fighting, bleeding, and weakening while she establishes her reign.

After the Iran-Iraq war, Saddam Hussein eradicated the cells of the Iraqi Shiite political parties that were related to Iran. The bulk of them fled to Iran where they found refuge, care, and military training. Most of them returned to Iraq after the American invasion, astonished by a victory achieved effortlessly and without resources or bloodshed on their part. They returned to Iraq after the Bush administration paved the way for a theocratic, terrorist state that commits atrocities and crimes under the protection of American forces.

Chapter 5, Saddam's Trial, provides more information about the intentional concealment by the American administration of facts about what has been happening in Iraq since the invasion. The occupation authority surrendered Saddam Hussein as a prisoner of war to terrorist groups from Iran, now called political parties, and to the Iraqi government that has proved to be totally subordinate to these terrorists. Scores of facts and circumstantial evidence point to a clandestine Iranian state within Iraq. Hence, Saddam's trial by these factions represents an immoral act and a legal violation by the Bush administration. It is astonishing that a country which supports so many human rights organizations would violate international law by surrendering Saddam Hussein to his foes. Irrespective of the crimes that are attributed to him, Saddam is a scapegoat, offered to entities that the United States has fought against in the past. The United Sates has no legitimate reason to participate in a sectarian war with roots several centuries old—the Sunni-Shiite war.

By partaking in this war, the United States gains the hatred of most of the Muslim world. The U.S. is seen to be settling an account with Saddam who it previously helped against Iran. The American forces don't grasp why they fight. They can't see the logic that connects this war to the security and interests of the American people. The Americans do not understand the minor extent of al-Qaeda in Iraq and the myth of Abu Musa'ab al-Zarqawi. What is the secret behind the increasing number of American soldiers that were killed recently? Why does Iran push the Americans to fight the Sunnis in Iraq, engendering the hatred of most Muslim countries? How does Iran plan to evict the American army from Iraq? Iran will need to evict the Americans to achieve its historic dream of controlling Iraq. Iraq has lost the elements of modernity and civilization that were not absent during Saddam's rule and has descended into the Dark Ages. I will also discuss the bizarre alliance between the Bush administration and Iran's followers in Iraq and Saddam's trial as the "completed mission" of George W. Bush—that is how he refers to the trial when he is trying to justify the present uncontrolled situation in Iraq.

2

The New Iraq, an Iranian Nuclear Bomb!

There has been much debate in the world about the war that the Bush administration, supported by the American neoconservative sector, has waged on Iraq. There is a massive amount of information on this dangerous and disastrous adventure—much of it conflicting. There is unanimity, however, about one thing—that it is unlike other wars, conflicts, and disputes in modern history. Many parties agree on the false premises of this war, on the lies told by George W. Bush and his group prior to, and after the war. We wonder why he continues to lie after the false reasons for waging this war have been discovered. The questions at the top of the list concern the nonexistent relationship between Saddam's regime and the al-Qaeda organization and the nonexistence of weapons of mass destruction in Iraq.

These issues were clear a few days after the fall of Baghdad. Nonetheless, the American president and his cabal of strategic planners chose to escape the reality. They did not reevaluate the new information in a thoughtful manner. Nor did they study the potential repercussions of invading a sensitive country such as Iraq. Iraq is strategically important to the security of the Arabic gulf region, which secures the energy for half the world's population. Iraq is also central to the security of the Middle East region, a region that has gone through a series of bloody conflicts between Arabs and Israelis over the past six decades. If left without a solution in which the whole world participates, this conflict will lead to a universal disaster that could destroy the accomplishments of human civilization. The most dangerous issue that has been ignored by the American administration is Iraq's neighbor, the Islamic Republic of Iran.

Iran was present from the first moment the American president thought of invading Iraq, a few days after the September 11, 2001 attacks on the U.S. Trade Center. Iran was able to penetrate the political decision-making circles in the

United States through her loyalists in the Shiite political parties that rule Iraq today. Iraqi Iranian agents have been the largest source of false information about Saddam's Iraq. They were successful in misleading the Bush administration into invading Iraq. Iran was able to pass exaggerated information through her agents in the Iraqi opposition to Saddam's regime. The Iranian plan to trick the United States into invading Iraq reflects the historic revenge of Shiites against Sunni Muslims. The political Islamic Shiite bloc led by Iran plotted to mislead the American administration to the point where it would sanction a war against Saddam Hussein. The Iranian plan was an attempt to take revenge against the Sunni Islamic countries that supported the 1980–1988 Iran-Iraq war.

The Bush administration was excited after the occupation of Iraq, celebrating a nonexistent victory and a battle that did not take place. There was no parity between American and Iraqi forces. In fact, Iraq had only the symbols of military units. Iraqi military units were empty of weapons, there was no preparation, and most of the military withdrew before the beginning of the war. The Bush administration wanted to save face by not pausing after the invasion so the world would not discover its mistake in waging the war. The consequences of America's mistake are grave—the United States, the Middle East, and the whole world face instability and conflict, and thus, great danger. Today Iraq supports expanding terrorist discourse and fanaticism and there is no indication that these threats will be neutralized soon. Explosions, random killings, religious sectarian kidnappings, and the severing of heads are performed by small, fanatic Sunni groups in today's Iraq. The Iranians and their Iraqi Shiite agents, however, have magnified the acts of these groups in order to persuade the American army to kill more Sunni Muslims. Meanwhile, Iranian intelligence has established prisons and secret centers inside Iraq to torture the former leadership of the Iraqi army that fought the war against Iran. The current situation in Iraq has led most Iraqis to make a comparison between today's situation and Saddam's dictatorship with all its craziness and horror. They are nostalgic for the ugly days of Saddam's reign because, unlike occupied Iraq, there was no lack of security.

The American president started his propaganda for the occupation a few days after the fall of Baghdad and the removal of Saddam, viewing it as a victory for mankind. Propaganda theorists of the neoconservative sector were successful in manipulating the narrow-minded American president. They urged him to visit the aircraft carrier, the U.S.S. Abraham Lincoln to address the military. On the carrier, Bush, dressed in a flight suit, announced the victory he had accomplished in Iraq. A banner behind the president read "Mission Accomplished." Ironically, any person with a minimum knowledge of military affairs would not describe what took place in Iraq as a military battle. The strongest military power in the world had attacked a devastated country—a country whose economy was in shambles as a result of international sanctions that had continued for more than a decade. There was no battle worth celebrating and the victory claimed by the American president was an illusion. Subsequently, this mock victory has been transformed into a strategic defeat and a glaring moral defeat for the American state. This is the view of many leading American intellectual and political figures such as Jimmy Carter. Bush's victory celebration was an episode in a series of escapist communications that the American administration has been delivering since the occupation of Iraq.

The Clandestine Iranian State in Iraq

The Islamic Republic of Iran celebrated the occupation of Iraq considering it a strategic, historic, and free victory. Iran is considered the real occupier of Iraq, as Iranian control in Iraq has benefited from the American occupation. The Iranians were thankful for a victory which had been delayed for more than 1400 years. That is the age of the Sunni-Shiite schism. A victory without battle, over Sunni Muslims who represent 85 percent of the Muslim world, had the flavor of being poured from heaven. The victory had been achieved through the American invasion of Iraq. Iraq was late to join the Ayat Allah al-Khomeini's empire by more than two decades. This was so because the world had stood against such a plan. When the simple Shiite people saw the American military pouring into the historical city of Baghdad, they visualized that as a blessing and victory from heaven to the soul of Ayat Allah al-Khomeini. The Shiites witnessed what they felt was a miracle. But the cost to the Americans was dear—in dollars, more than 400 billion—in soldiers, over twenty-five hundred, many of whom were killed or handicapped. In addition, the killing of hundreds of thousands of innocent Iraqi civilians aroused the hatred of about one billion Muslims. Moreover, the war was condemned by most of the world community. Claims such as the safeguarding of American national security, the democratizing of Iraq, advancing the front of the war on terror, and the mantra that American forces fight in Iraq so they will not be compelled to fight on the streets of American cities are all slogans dreamed up by George W. Bush and his neoconservative supporters to justify illegal aggression.

The American administration has used American soldiers' blood and American taxpayers' money to bolster its reputation and image. The Bush administration has embarked upon an immoral and deceptive mission that has no precedent in modern history. One consequence of American carelessness has been an enhanced capability of the Islamic Republic of Iran to establish a secret state in Iraq. This secret state is a threat to international peace and security. Where are the American security and intelligence agencies that are proud of their capability to detect the smallest object in our globe? The center of decision making in the American administration has shackled the country's capability to deal responsibly and cautiously with the situation in Iraq. This is a pitfall for any country where the political leadership dominates the state's apparatus.

Freedom has returned for loyalists of the Islamic Republic of Iran. The American occupation of Iraq released three decades of suppression and oppression by Saddam Hussein who abolished all pro-Iran religious political parties. The Iranian loyalists started their activity one day after the American forces entered Baghdad. One day after the fall of Baghdad, Sastani, the spiritual leader of the Iraqi Shiites, issued an important *fatwa* to the grass roots of the Khomeinian political parties in Iraq. He cautioned them to not engage in hostilities against the American forces or the occupation authority. Moreover, he ordered them to cooperate temporarily with the American forces. Sastani wanted to settle scores with Iran's foes and rivals in other sects and organizations in Iraq. He did not want to panic the American forces who were now in an alien land, ignorant of its geography and the complexion of its people. However, the Iraqi people started a legitimate resistance when confronted by unjustified foreign invasion. The object of Sastani's *fatwa* was the destruction of historical foes and the socialist secular loyalists of Saddam Hussein. At the same time, Iran wanted the United States to be implicated in crimes and violations against the Iraqi people—charges that could be used against the United States later, after Iranian dominance of the Iraqi state.

Iran has been successful on two fronts. Iran and her Iraqi agents eliminated their historical enemy, courtesy of the American army. And Iran has achieved complete dominance over Iraq as a result of a mixture of issues involving the American administration that resulted in a dangerous power imbalance in favor of Iran. Currently Iran is a major terrorist state that represents a threat to international security. In order for the political situation in this important region of the world to return to its preinvasion status—and for a return to the preinvasion strategic map—unusual efforts are needed. The security of the Middle East region is dangerously close to spinning out of control. The ramifications of that event would be world-wide. The international community faces the twin challenges of dismantling the secret Iranian state that dominates Iraq and reorganizing Iraq's internal affairs. A stable Iraq will be achieved only without the dominance of religious and sectarian political parties.

While the Bush administration was engaged in a sectarian war, settling a score between Sunni and Shiite Muslims in Iraq, Iran progressed with its nuclear program. The outcome of the Iraqi invasion was quite different from what had been visualized by the Bush administration. Rather than securing its own interests, the invasion by the United States transformed Iraq into a strategic weapon for Iran. The hegemony Iran gained over the state apparatus of Iraq, including its security, parliament, and the army, has given Iran the power to offer Iraq in exchange for negotiating Iran's nuclear program. This puts the American administration in a complex and embarrassing situation. Furthermore, Iran has begun to exploit its total dominance of Iraq to impose its will on the entire world.

In the current scenario, any attempt to deal militarily with Iran by the United States or any other party would most likely lead to a universal or semi-universal conflict. So a military option is not under consideration. Iran is capable of mobilizing millions of armed Iraqi Shiites against the American forces in Iraq if the United States resorts to tougher measures to deal with the Iranian nuclear program. Thus the American adventure in Iraq and its consequences are put into perspective. The situation has crippled the ability of the United States and the international community to deal with the Iranian danger that escalates daily.

Within this context, the Iranian president has threatened to wipe Israel from the world map. The highly sensitive Palestinian question is the principal conundrum of the Muslim world. There is unanimity that the Palestinian issue will not be settled through fundamentalist discourse—Israeli or Muslim. Perhaps the Iranian threat to wipe Israel from the map is a message to the fanatic Israelis who supported the false and illegitimate war on Iraq. The new Iraq represents a much more potent danger to future peace in the Middle East. There exist covert channels of communication between Israel and the Iraqi Shiite political parties, and from time-to-time the Shiites deliver indirect assurances to Israel, yet in the end the Shiites are part and parcel of the strategy of the Islamic Republic of Iran. The future may see an Iraqi nuclear program supported by Iran; at the very least we can imagine Iraq stockpiling nuclear weapons for Iran or becoming a passageway for Iran's nuclear technology. Hence, the false claim of weapons of mass destruction used by the American administration as justification for the invasion of Iraq might become a reality. At the moment, the American administration is too busy fighting the civilian Iraqis to pay attention to such a scenario. Even if it did, what could it do about it? It is fair to say the American administration has placed the entire world in a precarious situation by its ill-conceived adventures in Iraq.

Iran's Strategy to Evict the American Army from Iraq

For a long time, American forces in Iraq were engaged in following a myth magnified by Iranian intelligence. Iranian intelligence issued many statements in the name of al-Zarqawi and followers of several other small, fanatic Sunni groups to intimidate and distract the American forces. Iran and her loyalists in the Iraqi government are still magnifying al-Qaeda's role in Iraq to the same purpose. This strategy resulted in disproportionate attacks on Sunni cities and villages by American forces. The Iranians and Shiite ruling political parties exploit the state of Islam phobia that prevails in the American armed forces, especially in the young soldiers who consider all Sunni Iraqis to be supporters of al-Qaeda. It is worth mentioning that al-Qaeda has no grassroot popularity in Iraq or in the Muslim world and I will deal with this serious issue in another book. Since September 11, 2001, al-Qaeda, has been exploited by many to manipulate the behavior of their opponents. Iran and her Iraqi loyalists have the right to be proud of their participation in this goal.

While the Americans were engaged in hostilities against the Iraqis, Iran decided to introduce measures to force the American administration to withdraw its forces from Iraq. It started by spreading propaganda against the American occupation directed toward public opinion in Iraq, the Arab world, and the Muslim world. The medium was a television station, al-A'alam, a political station that airs in Arabic and was established by the Iranian intelligence immediately after the American occupation. Al-A'alam concentrates on American forces' violations and abuses. Iran, through her Iraqi allies, has played a vital role in publicizing abuses and violations of American forces. Iran's motive is to weaken the American forces and force them to make an unplanned withdrawal, paving the way for the great Khomeinian empire to take over.

They Kill American Soldiers

Iranians have established secret arms stockpiles all over Iraq. They also have secret prisons, some of which were discovered by the Americans in November 2005. This framework, constructed by Iranian intelligence, has benefited from the state of apparent unconsciousness of American intelligence organs in Iraq. Iranians have also gained control of all Iraqi embassies. The source of danger here is that the Islamic Republic of Iran, isolated since its birth in 1979, now has more than a 100,000 passports and other Iraqi documents obtained from agents in the al-Jaa'fari government. Hence, Iran is capable of spying on Iranian freedom fighters (and of assassinating them) all over the world.

Using false Iraqi documents, the Iranian death squad moves freely in the world looking for potential victims among those who oppose the Iranian regime. Iran has a long legacy of practicing such assassination and terror. Most of the Iraqi diplomatic corps overseas are members of the political cadre of Iraqi Shiites ideologically linked to Iran. Therefore the assistance and coordination they provide to the Iraqi government is strongly aligned with the agendas of Shiite political parties who cooperate with Iran.

The dominance of Shiite political parties in the Iraqi government is due to the under-representation of Kurds and the weakness of Jalal al-Talabani, the Iraqi president, who also has close ties with Iran. His office is only nominal with very limited responsibilities and cannot influence Iranian policies in Iraq. His foreign minister, a Kurdish technocrat who opposed Saddam Hussein, has limited political experience compared to the new foreign ministry officials who are in the cadre of Shiite political parties. These Shiite parties underwent military training in the Revolutionary Guards camps in Iran, and their first allegiance is to their ideological and sectarian loyalties rather than to the nation. This is a real problem for the Iraqi social fabric because the Iraqi Shiites prioritize Iran's interests rather than Iraq's. During the Iran-Iraq war most of them fought on the Iranian side. That is why Saddam Hussein was harsh in dealing with them and their case is now the first among others against him in the court proceedings now underway. Iraqi diplomatic missions and embassies have become a threat to international peace and security because they are used by Iran to target prodemocracy Iranians.

The killing of American soldiers in Iraq accelerated between August and November 2005, the time of writing this manuscript. This coincided with two issues: the tension caused by the Iranian nuclear program—which frightens the whole international community, and the Iranian call for American withdrawal—an intense political campaign and propaganda against American forces' violations. The propaganda calling for American withdrawal has been orchestrated through the al-A'alam television station and sponsored by Iranian intelligence. Iranian intelligence routinely uses al-A'alam to spread its spying activities in Iraq and elsewhere under the guise of media business. Experts in Iraqi affairs, who are familiar with the size and composition of the Iraqi resistance, suggest that Iran is a direct partner in the ever-increasing killing of American soldiers. This implies that the Iraqi state apparatus, comprised of Shiite Iraqis, provides detailed information on American forces' logistics, and that the betrayal of American "friends" is organized by Iranian intelligence. That is how the Iraqi government covertly contributes to the killing of American soldiers. Also to be considered: there is an undeclared front on Basra between the British army and the local Iraqi government that is related to Iran.

For Iran and her Iraqi followers, the American phase in Iraq is over. They kill American soldiers to compel the American forces to leave Iraq. The American reaction to these killings is foolish—attacks on and bombardment of Sunni villages and cities. These vengeful attacks, coupled with the destruction of civilian buildings, have been shown in the world (including Muslim and Arab) media. Victims of these attacks include children and innocent Sunni civilians, which increases Muslim and Arab hatred of America and enhances the discourse among fanatic groups. Such attacks encourage the frustrated youth to join these fanatic groups. The targeting of civilians in Iraq harms Western interests and makes Western citizens targets for random killing world-wide. This is exactly what was planned and is being achieved effortlessly by Iran. This is what the American president and his administration have accomplished—they have made the world more dangerous and less peaceful.

What is now needed in Iraq is an impartial and neutral international investigation of the history and sequence of events that have led to its current situation. This is something the traditional international mechanism, such as the United Nations cannot deal with. The U.N. has been unable to achieve the objectives enshrined in its charter because it is subordinate to the American administration—the very administration that caused the current problems in Iraq. The precarious situation in Iraq and its threat to regional and international peace necessitates a nontraditional solution planned and executed by the international community. Participation must include those who opposed the Iraqi invasion and others with related policies from Iraq and other countries. There must be no intervention by the United States as it is not a neural party. This is a remote probability because of the known American arrogance, yet the abovementioned scenario is the only solution that will avoid a huge universal conflict that starts in Iraq.

3

Saddam Hussein—His Beginning and his End

Saddam Hussein, now on trial for crimes to humanity, has been and is one of the world's most controversial figures. From the 1950s he has played a significant role in Iraq's contemporary political history and in the world at large. Whether executed or not, he will remain a controversial figure, forever remembered, particularly by Arabs and Muslims.

Saddam Hussein joined the Arab Socialist Ba'th party at a young age. In the late 1950s, the military-oriented Ba'th party assigned Saddam and a group of his comrades to assassinate president Abel-Karim Qasim, a communist general. The mission failed and Saddam was wounded. Saddam went underground in Iraq to avoid the secret police, then fled to Syria and from there to Egypt where he lived as a political refugee and started studying law. After two years, Saddam discontinued his study and returned to Iraq when a military coup, organized by the Ba'th party, took place in 1963. General Qasim was killed in this coup. The situation remained unstable as a result of differences among the Ba'thist groups and Saddam was part of a group expelled from the Ba'thist party. Again he returned to a life of fleeing, jails, and hiding.

Saddam's First Steps to Power

In 1968, the Ba'thist group to which Saddam belonged staged a military coup by which it assumed power; Saddam became the second man in the Iraqi Revolutionary Command Council (RCC), the supreme authority in the country. He began building a closed circle of influence in the Ba'th party as well as the RCC. Within a short time Saddam developed a fearful personality and established his influence in the army and intelligence. While he was the second man in the regime, he dealt with those who didn't agree with him very harshly. Because President Ahmed al-Bakr was in bad health, Saddam took responsibility for major decisions. This situation continued until 1979 when President al-Bakr resigned and Saddam became president of the Republic of Iraq.

Saddam began his regime with a massacre. His method was typically Ba'thist—he called some conspirators to a meeting and had them executed as they arrived. Saddam was practicing party procedure for dealing with opponents and rivals who opposed Ba'th policies. Saddam's regime was successful in achieving economic and social development and a reputable health care system. However, his achievements suffered from his propensity to take all major decisions alone. One such decision was his reckless invasion of Kuwait in 1990. He sent one million soldiers, most from the irregular army, to invade Kuwait; they did anarchic deeds there. When he invaded Kuwait, Saddam had just concluded an eight-year war with Iran that had drained Iraqi resources. The occupation of Kuwait dealt a heavy blow to his regime for it was followed by long economic sanctions that continued until the American occupation in March 2003.

The American Invasion, Baghdad's Fall, and Saddam's Capture

The September 11, 2001 attacks on the United States resulted in a rush by American neoconservatives to implement a grand but unrealistic project—a project to control and reshape the Middle East by means of propaganda and force. Iraq was at the top of the project's list; the project began and died in Iraq.

Prior to the invasion of Iraq, the American administration unleashed a frenzy of propaganda dedicated to preparing the American public for its goal of transforming the Middle East starting with Iraq. Saddam did not have enough military power to withstand an American invasion, but he appeared determined to defend his dignity, refusing the American ultimatum to leave Iraq along with his family within 24 hours. Saddam ignored the official invitations of many Arab and European countries to arrange his peaceful exit from Iraq. He chose to remain in his homeland and face a war that would have no parity. In fact, Saddam was clinging to his family, clan, and Arab tradition that considers surrender to an enemy shameful. He disregarded offers made that were acceptable to America, including one made by the late Zayd bin Sultan, the leader of the U.A.E. Instead, he chose to follow Arab tradition.

Saddam remained in Baghdad, trying to resist and hoping to inflict heavy losses on invading forces that were advancing quickly toward the capital city. The military weight on either side was wildly disproportional. American tanks were pouring into Baghdad through many entrances on the day it fell. By that time Saddam was keen to make a public appearance in Baghdad. It was his last appearance as leader of Iraq. Later, Saddam's sons Uday and Qusay and his 14 year-old grandson were killed by American forces that destroyed their hiding place. Their bodies were disfigured and the American occupational authority decided to keep the incident secret.

After Saddam's last appearance he disappeared and many rumors circulated about his whereabouts. Some speculated that he had fled to neighboring Syria, others that he was in Russia. In the aftermath of a victory that had been accomplished without a battle, the American forces distributed a list of the most wanted political players with Saddam as number one. From his miserable hiding place Saddam continued to send messages to the Iraqi people; some of which were aired by al-Jazeera, the Arab news network. The ease with which the Iraqi leadership was captured suggested that they had not arranged an underground plan before the invasion. Saddam, who had experience in underground maneuvers, was caught in a miserable bunker after the death of his sons and grandson. Saddam had spent years successfully eluding the secret police—it is hard to see how he could have been captured without a betrayal. Perhaps those who were in touch with him felt burdened by him or decided to disclose his whereabouts seeking the price on his head. This is the most logical interpretation. Other versions, such as the story that the Americans arrested him a long time before and brought him under anesthesia into the bunker were flights of imagination—a kind of condolence for the broken heart of the average Arab. Whatever may have been the mistakes of the former president and the grievances held by the populace, the appearance of Saddam when he was captured was humiliating and hurtful to the Arab world.

Saddam's Trial and the Iran-America Deal

The American administration was disillusioned in its daydream of Iraqis welcoming the American troops. Caught in failure when Baghdad streets were transformed into moving sand, unhinging American soldiers and disabling their machinery, the American administration resorted to the propaganda that terrorist groups were leading the resistance in Iraq. Both the authority of American occupation and Iraqi Shiite political parties perpetrated this myth. Amidst this campaign came the issue of Saddam's trial when the occupation authority turned him over to the pro-Iran government.

On June 30, 2003 the prisoner of war, Saddam Hussein, was transferred to the custody of the Iraqi transitional government appointed by the Governing Council headed by Paul Bremer. Saddam was now at the mercy of his historical enemy, a point that annuls the claim that the court was impartial. This was confirmed later when he was deprived of his status as a prisoner of war. The Bush administration surrendered Saddam's right as a prisoner of war as quid pro quo in a deal to appease the Iraqi sectarian government that regularly receives guidance from Tehran. The Iraqi and Iranian governments coordinate with each other on all delicate issues under the American occupation.

Saddam's trial went through different phases. Inexperienced judges headed the initial phase; most of them were public relations officers that were related to international intelligence circles. The last phase began in March 2006. Pressures and sectarian terrorism accompanied this trial and worked together to project it into the form of the infamous Iranian revolutionary courts. As a consequence, the Kurdish judge, Rarkaz Amin, resigned, justifying his resignation by citing political interference. This interference coincided with terrorist actions executed by Iranian intelligence and the Shiite militias that killed two defense lawyers and other co-defenders. A judge who bears personal malice because he was a former political detainee during the Saddam regime was substituted for Rarkaz Amin. This implies that he was chosen to make sure Saddam will be executed. A predetermined regulation stated that the verdict must be reached within 30 days with no right for the defender to appeal.

The trial of Saddam Hussein, from its first day, resembled a play with a very unskilled director. A minor case was chosen amidst very serious and major cases such as the Iran-Iraq war, the invasion of Kuwait, and the subsequent gulf war. The defendant involved in these cases ruled his country for more than two decades. Therefore, all these cases are related to each other and it is impossible to achieve any measure of impartiality and justice if one is tried separately. The exclusion of any of these cases indicates concealment of the American role in Saddam's wars, for he was a part of the American strategy when American and Iraqi interests overlapped to face the Shiite tide in the aftermath of the Khomeini revolution in 1979. The trial proceedings proved that there was a silent deal between Iran and the American administration by which the latter remained silent about the way in which Saddam's trial was conducted, whether or not the verdict is execution.

If Saddam is executed, what does the sectarian government in Baghdad lose? Nothing, because the trial has been in harmony with justice according to Khomeini and Islamic revolutionary courts. However, the responsibility lies with the American administration. The main case that has been dealt with so far is the execution of over one hundred Iraqis after the pro-Iran al-Da'wa cadre tried to assassinate Saddam Hussein during his visit to a village called al-Dejail. It has been proved that the plot was planned by Iranian intelligence during the Iran-Iraq War.

Execution or Exile?

As mentioned earlier, Saddam's execution is something sacred for the Shiite *huza* that currently rules both Iran and Iraq. Neither Iran nor the Iraqi political parties would feel any embarrassment if Saddam was executed in a hurried way. He would be a victim of the current American administration. At the same time he would be transformed from a socialist and failed dictator into a patriotic and Islamic *mujahid*. Thousands of poems would be composed for him. He would be an Islamic symbol and one of the martyrs of the American design in Arab and Muslim worlds. We would be reminded of other leaders who chose to not revolve in the American orbit and met horrific assassinations: Lumumba of the Congo, the Bolivian revolutionary Che Guevara, the elected Chilean president Salvador Allende. Moreover, Saddam's execution would, even for those who had differences with him, be seen as another case of the American administration misleading the American people. Saddam has been offered as a scapegoat in an undeclared Iranian-American deal. The Saddam case is one of many complex issues between Tehran and Washington such as the Iranian nuclear program and Iran's influence in Iraq and Lebanon. There is a remote possibility that international or American intervention could save him from his historical enemies.

4

The Trial and Execution of Saddam Hussein—The America-Iran Deal

Saddam Hussein's trial represents a peak of American violation and aggression in Iraq. American transgressions in Iraq that led up to the trial include the invasion and illegitimate occupation of Iraq. This occupation has resulted in complete Iranian hegemony over Iraq. It is public opinion in Islamic and Arab countries that the trial of Saddam Hussein represents an episode in a series of aggressions directed against the Islamic world by the American administration. Yesterday's Saddam is not today's Saddam. He has been transformed through his trial into a figure of greater proportion than that of a former ruler of Iraq with a legacy of terror. However, the Muslim people question why Saddam was not tried in a legitimate international court such as the one that was provided to the former Yugoslavian president Milosevic, although he killed and eradicated tens of thousands of Muslims in the Balkans. Milosevic was tried by the International Criminal Court of war criminals in The Hague and privileged with legal and secure protection, and his human dignity was respected, something that the American administration, which claims to be a guardian of human rights, did not provide to the Muslim and Arab president Saddam Hussein.

Mr. Hussein's dignity and rights have been violated scores of times by the authority of the occupation that intentionally humiliated him in an inhuman and uncivilized manner; for instance, when he was shown in the media in his underwear. Moreover, this authority failed to protect Saddam Hussein from a member of a sectarian militia who assaulted him in the courtroom and did not provide protection to his lawyers, some of whom were assassinated by the militia of the Iranian political parties that dominate Iraq. People question why the Bush administration handed over a prisoner of war to the Iraqi government that is known to be loyal and tied to the theocratic, sectarian state Iran. All these are

21

legitimate questions. However, the worse thing about Hussein's trial is that, in a public address heard by the entire world before the beginning of the trial, the American president George W. Bush said that Mr. Hussein deserved the death penalty. Also before the trial, the Iranian government submitted an official application to the new Iraqi government to include the Iran-Iraq war of 1980–1988 in the case against Saddam Hussein. It was the Bush administration that put Saddam Hussein at the mercy of his Iraqi and Iranian foes. Is this American justice?

Among the charges against the former Iraqi president is the murdering of citizens of an Iraqi locality called al-Dejail during the Iran-Iraq war after some pro-Iran citizens of that locality attacked his parade. Most of Saddam's victims during that era were soldiers in the Iranian army and members of Iraqi religious political parties known to be loyal to Iran and its fanatic leader Ayat Allah al-Khomeini. To reach the truth about what was taking place in Iraq during the Iran-Iraq war, what is needed is the establishment of a legal and impartial court. The fact that the U.S. was a partner in the war against Iran should be considered in the case against Saddam; also, other Saddam adventures in which the United States of America was an essential player should be documented in the trial. It is astonishing that the Iraqi government that tries Saddam has resorted to ghost witnesses who testify behind a curtain. The identity of those witnesses is unknown and their statements were weak and they contradicted themselves, an indication that most of their statements had been dictated to them before the trial. It looks as though there is a predetermined plan to find a verdict of guilty followed by a sentence of capital punishment. This conclusion has already been arrived at in Iraqi circles affiliated to Iran.

The trial of Saddam Hussein, the former Iraqi president, takes place in a country where explosions and suicide bombers are the norm. It takes place in a country where secret detention centers and torture are common and the citizens are dominated by militias. The violence spread by those militias is echoed in the courtroom where Saddam Hussein and seven of his aides are being tried for war crimes. The principal judge of this court has been pressured with threats to conclude the process swiftly and announce the execution of Saddam Hussein. While the trial was in progress, pro-Iran Shiite militia assassinated two of the defense lawyers. This led to the resignation of the sitting judge. Another judge was appointed. The *Suabiqa* newspaper said the new judge had been appointed to accomplish what Iran and the ruling Shiite Iraqis wish for, that is, to execute Saddam Hussein. This would fit the fanatic pattern of the Shiite political parties who would be following an old *fatwa* issued by Imam al-Khomeini to kill or execute Saddam Hussein by any means. This story is commonly narrated on the streets of

Iran and Iraq and the opportunity to implement this sacred command has been passed to Khomeini followers.

Saddam has become a controversial issue to people in the Middle East. Some see his trial as a trial of Arabs and Muslims; some see his execution as a victory in the Sunni-Shiite conflict. The American occupation uses Saddam's trial to pressurize Iran's pursuit of nuclear weapons. The claim that Saddam's trial is an Iraqi issue lacks honesty and accuracy. The American administration chooses who governs Iraq under a shadow of a pseudodemocratic practice. Only the American administration has the power to try Saddam Hussein. Thus, the Bush administration could threaten Iran by saving Saddam's life as a means to terrorize agents of the Iranian project in Iraq. Or Saddam can be sacrificed to appease the Iranian Iraqi Shiite *huza* so it will not engage in confrontations with the forces of the American occupation. It is most likely that the American administration will give the green light to execute Saddam Hussein in the framework of an Iranian-American deal through an Iraqi middleman. Even though the United States of America is absent in Saddam's trial and satisfied by his imprisonment, it was a partner in managing his previous conflicts with Iran and his victims in Iraqi Shiite political parties who are now the main issue in his indictment.

Probably the simplest principles of justice necessitate the provision of a neutral trial for Saddam Hussein so that the world can reach an informed conclusion that the accusation that he committed crimes against humanity is justifiable. However, the United States avoids a neutral trial for it would expose the American role in Saddam's misadventures to the world community. A neutral trial would also reveal that most of Saddam's victims were not civilian citizens but ideological fighters belonging to religious Iraqi political parties that carried arms against their own country to support the Iranian revolution led by the extremist Ayat Allah al-Khomeini. A neutral trial for Saddam Hussein would demonstrate to the world community that the exploitation of simple people in religious wars and ideological conflicts can be punished. Such a lesson might help mankind avoid similar conflicts.

In the Iran-Iraq war, misled innocents were not fighting a dictator, they were fighting the infidel ruler, Saddam Hussein, who did not follow the *sharia* laws. They considered that fighting Saddam was sufficient reason to enter into paradise and that Ayat Allah al-Khomeini was providing the keys. Those who fought the war against Saddam Hussein were fighting for religious reasons, not for democracy as they and the Bush administration claim. During the Iraq-Iran war, the United States supported Saddam Hussein to deter the Khomeini revolution. The Iraqi offspring of this war are George W. Bush's current allies who rule Iraq now.

Saddam's trial should have included many accused besides Saddam Hussein and the former Iraqi leadership. At the top of the list would be those that have engaged in local and international terror. For example, the Shiite Iraqi leader Ali al-Sastani, the de facto ruler of the American Iraq, who is of Iranian origin, recruited and misled simple people to wage religious war. Other examples are the current Iraqi prime minister and the leadership of the religious political parties that rule Iraq today through American assistance. These are foes of Saddam Hussein and have fought a long war against him as followers of Ayat Allah al-Khomeini. It is interesting to note that under the protection of the American forces, Ibrahim al-Jaa'fari, the Iraqi prime minister, has visited and kissed Khomeini's tomb believing that Khomeini was a holy man who received revelation from Allah. In a neutral trial there would be more than one impartial witness to enhance the pillars of justice. Participants in Saddam's trial, that is, the American administration, the Shiite political parties, and the Iranian government are not above suspicion; that is why they chose this fast and revengeful trial with a verdict issued before its commencement. Thus, Saddam's trial sets a shameful but unique precedent in the legacy of international law.

Many documentaries report events during Saddam Hussein's regime that could constitute major cases against him. These documentaries are available in the American media and elsewhere in the world. They could have helped constitute a pillar of justice, had they been uncensored, by relating the history of Saddam's reign, including events in the Iran-Iraq war. They would have explained what was taking place in Iraq during that era with legal authority. Instead, political immoral authority has prevailed, mixing issues and evading laws to produce an exchange of roles between the pro-Iran Iraqi government and the American administration. In Saddam's trial the interests of the American administration overlap those of Iran. There is no interpretation for such overlap apart from a deal in which the Bush administration offers Saddam's head as a price to appease the Khomeinians who now rule Iraq as well as Iran.

In footage shown by the American media, Iraqi forces belonging to Saddam's regime brutally execute a number of followers of the Shiite political parties loyal to Iran. This event took place in 1990 when the U.S. was trying to evict Iraqi forces from Kuwait in the aftermath of the war waged by the United States on Iraq. The Shiite forces exploited the state of war and the anarchy that prevailed in Iraq and occupied a number of Iraqi cities in accordance with orders issued by Iran. At that time, Iran exploited the situation by using the mob to take over power after an anticipated collapse of Saddam's regime in wake of the deterioration of his forces in Kuwait and inside Iraq.

However, the American military's field leadership received orders to immediately withdraw from the highways that led to the Shiite rebellion as well as from centers of the remaining Iraqi army. It was a clear message from the American leadership represented by George Bush Sr., the father of George W. Bush, to Saddam Hussein to do whatever he liked with the rebellious Shiites. Saddam grasped the message, moved his forces, and crushed the Shiite rebellion brutally. A few hours after this massacre, an American television station interviewed George Bush Sr., who was playing golf as if nothing had happened. Asked why he did not interfere to stop the massacre, he replied calmly that the American forces were not there to intervene; he stated that America had a specific mission to evict Saddam Hussein and liberate Kuwait, and that had been accomplished. What he didn't say was that those Shiite rebels might have established a government loyal to Iran and this would have been disastrous to American strategy in this region. It would have been better had the Iranian loyalists established a government in Iraq in 1990, for in 2005 George W. Bush has generously offered Iraq as a gift to Iran. And now it is a gift enriched by the blood of thousands of American soldiers and its price has been paid by American taxpayers.

A neutral trial for Saddam Hussein might have been an opportunity to explore the role played by the United States of America in the events for which he is being tried today. The Bush administration has intentionally evaded this investigation in arranging the trial of the former Iraqi president. I anticipate Saddam's trial and its consequences to be a historical trial of the Bush administration that will take years to reach a conclusion. Saddam Hussein will be a living legend in the Arab and Islamic world, perhaps in the whole world if he is executed. The execution of Saddam Hussein is anticipated by those who set up the trial, but they may not appreciate the myth they are creating.

The execution of Saddam Hussein will not change the political balance in Iraq and the Middle East region except to add more destruction to Iraq and enhance terror. It will be a spiritual victory for the Khomeinians. The United States of America will have a hard time defending its reputation as a state that claims to protect freedom and democracy after the imbroglio in Iraq—having caused an escalation of the sectarian war between Shiite and Sunni Iraqis.

On the other hand, Saddam's execution under the American hegemony over Iraq will enhance fundamentalist discourse. Al-Qaeda will be especially glad to see him executed because he is a historical enemy of Islamic political groups in their various forms. Nonetheless, al-Qaeda and other fundamentalist groups will utilize an execution verdict politically, religiously, and for propaganda purposes to the maximum extent. These groups will portray the execution of Saddam as a crime against Muslims and Arabs rather than against the former president of Iraq. Western interests, particularly American, will be affected in the Middle East and other parts of the globe. Iran will come out on top because for the second time it has dragged the United States of America into a long and exhausting war of attrition with extremist groups.

Saddam's trial will end on the Iranian Iraqi gallows. However, the political assassination of a former state president will continue to be a subject of criticism for many generations to come. The existence of sufficient material evidence to implicate the United States and its Iranian ally in war crimes in Iraq will fuel debate long after the execution of Saddam Hussein. It is worth mentioning that Saddam's trial did not include the only case for which he cannot defend himself, the occupation of Kuwait. During the occupation of Kuwait, many Kuwaitis were killed, services were destroyed, and the Kuwaiti economy suffered enormous losses—this constitutes a full-fledged case against Saddam. However, the Kuwaiti people and their political leadership are convinced that Saddam's trial is taking place in a framework of plans unrelated to the achievement of justice, peace, and the establishment of democracy in Iraq and the Middle East. Thus, Kuwait is not enthusiastic to include its case for the time being.

The escalation of violence and possible disruption of world peace might be avoided if the American administration evaluates the situation in Iraq more carefully. The senseless killing of Iraqi Sunnis is a result of American observance of deceptive Iranian policy. This policy is skillfully executed by the Iraqi Shiite political parties that are affiliated with Iran and has been precisely planned to propel the United States into a war of attrition with the Sunni Muslim world. So far it has been utterly successful.

Under the current Bush administration, the U.S. has lost its allies and strategic partners in the Islamic and Arab worlds. Countries such as Egypt, Saudi-Arabia, and the gulf states are not satisfied with American policies for dealing with Middle Eastern affairs, although they don't voice these concerns to preserve protocol. America needs all the cooperation it can get from Middle Eastern countries if it is to resolve the conflict in Iraq and deal with the Iranian nuclear threat. Any attempt to deal with adverse effects of the war on Iraq without participation of these countries will be a total failure.

The American administration needs to return to judiciousness and immediately revoke all mistaken and destructive decisions that it issued in the aftermath of the invasion of Iraq. An example of a destructive decision was the dissolution of the Iraqi army. The American administration should hold direct negotiations with the former leadership of the Iraqi army. It also must release the previous

Iraqi leadership and arrange a comprehensive Iraqi reconciliation conference to be hosted by an Arabic capital. The structure of the new army and security forces has to be set up on a national base rather than the current one controlled by the Iranian sectarian faction.

However, such actions will lead to an open confrontation with the pro-Iran leadership of the Shiite Iraqis, that is, the Shiite *huza,* the de facto ruler of Iraq, to which the current Iraqi government has limitless loyalty. This religious *huza* is biotically related to the Islamic Republic of Iran that is running against time to force the American army to withdraw from Iraq in order to enhance its hegemony over this strategic region. This is the situation. George W. Bush has to for once be honest with his people and the world. He faces tremendous pressure from his people to withdraw American forces from Iraq. He suspects that the American people are aware of the mistake he made invading Iraq, looking for weapons of mass destruction, since there were no such weapons found. At the same time, George W. Bush worries about Iranian hegemony over Iraq, and the information he receives from the Shiite Iraqi political parties who dominate the region is biased by Iranian objectives. His own people are divided: some say he should withdraw the troops and cut his losses, some say he should increase the troops and finish the job he started. It is hard to determine whether the American public would support a large increase in American military strength in Iraq, so the latter may not be an option. Finally, we can say that any unstudied withdrawal of American forces from Iraq will benefit Iran. However, to remain in Iraq without altering the strategy of dependence on Shiite political parties and Iran's aides will continue the bloodshed and wastage of American resources without any gains. Moreover, every day the U.S. remains in Iraq increases the hatred of Islamic countries that are appalled by the killing of Sunni Muslims by the American-Iranian-Iraqi alliance.

5

Saddam's Trial: Facts and Documents

The trial of the former Iraqi president Saddam Hussein takes place in a tense international environment. World security is being eroded from several directions. The recent aggravation of terrorism in its different forms has made travel difficult and staying home uncertain. Global warming is beginning to look like a real threat and energy resources are becoming scarce. Mother Nature, ever eager to remind humanity of its vulnerability, is unleashing her usual calamities: floods, hurricanes, earthquakes, and has outdone herself by releasing several new generations of diseases and viruses faster than the international community can deal with them. In the midst of these global trials, the United States, under the leadership of George W. Bush, embarked on its misadventure in Iraq. Indifferent to international law and deaf to rational voices, the president of the United States pursued a plan of aggression which undermined world safety. Even now he ignores the threat of Iran's nuclear program in order to pursue an illusive victory over nonexistent enemies. Iran's nuclear program will have potentially disastrous consequences unless dealt with in a more judicious and prudent way.

Today, much information is available on the relationship between Saddam Hussein and several American government agencies. There are documents that cover strategic and security coordination with Saddam's regime and details of how the United States provided him with weapons and logistics during his war with Iran. These documents have now been released by the American government. They cover events such as the al-Dejail incident that were integral to the charges against Saddam in his trial. Al-Dejail was a military operation organized by Iranian intelligence and executed by Iraqi cadres of one of the fanatic religious political parties that rules Iraq today by American assistance. The Bush administration now uses American taxpayers' money to establish an Iranian entity in Iraq that dictates the trial of the former Iraqi president.

The trial of Saddam Hussein has witnessed events that have made modern history. The Shiite militias that belong to the terrorist Badr organization chased and killed two of Mr. Hussein's defense lawyers. The new Iraqi political leadership, which assumed power by means of American blood and money, has pressurized the judge to shorten the trial's time and sign a verdict. It is a verdict that has already been issued by the Iranian Shiite *huza*—to execute Saddam Hussein in response to the will of the fanatic Ayat Allah al-Khomeini who recommended assassinations of Saddam and his successor.

Most of the documents mentioned in this chapter confirm that the United States government is the prime witness absent from Saddam's trial. No one apart from the United States government can unveil what took place during Saddam's long rule, especially with regard to the use of chemical weapons against the people of the Kurdish city Halabja. Although Saddam is the prime suspect in this case, there are many who think that Iran rather than Saddam used chemical weapons in Halabja during the Iran-Iraq war. Many authorities and researchers who study the history of that era doubt that Saddam committed that heinous massacre. Several intelligence and legal experts share this viewpoint. They question why the United States remained silent when the Halabja massacre took place and why it continued its military cooperation with Saddam Hussein after this massacre.

The abovementioned observations confirm that the sectarian court that tries the former Iraqi president is not concerned with achieving justice. Rather, it seeks revenge on targets beyond Saddam and his regime's symbols. There is widespread feeling that this is a false court established on a false foundation, that is, the illegitimate occupation of Iraq. What is wanted is a separate and much larger trial of the American occupation of Iraq, its destructive consequences, and those who participated in it. The occupation's consequences are a series of horrible and unprecedented crimes that exacerbated conflicts in the Middle East region and beyond. Saddam's trial is almost a formality because he is already considered to be dead.

The sectarian trial of Mr. Hussein coincides with a major sectarian and civil war taking place in Iraq. The American administration has been party to this war from the first day of the occupation of Iraq. The recent American attempt to dismantle the institutions of the clandestine Iranian state in Iraq came too late. Such an attempt cannot achieve its goals because the pro-Iran Shiite establishment changed its tactics and strategy to cope with the new American plan. In particular, Iran has been successful in drawing the Bush administration further into the Iraqi quagmire and tries to join the nuclear club as the greatest regional power.

Iran also wants to negotiate Iraq's future with the United States. Saddam Hussein has become a trivial matter among these complicated issues. The Iranian hegemony and American occupation met to share the future of Iraq, including Saddam who has been transformed from a fearful figure that created important issues into a mere deal waiting for settlement between the fanatic American right-wing and Iranian Ayatollahs who virtually control Iraq.

Saddam's Trial? or Muslims and Arabs' Trial?

The trial of Saddam Hussein, the former Iraqi leader, has caused embarrassment for the so-called defenders and activists of international justice among the intellectual and political Western elite, in addition to several American and Western human rights organizations. The bulk of them do not have the courage to denounce the way in which Saddam's trial is being conducted. This trial has caused a huge theoretical debate for international law experts. Some of them criticize the way in which the trial takes place and forget the central issue, that is, the American occupation as an illegitimate and immoral deed and its impact. The consequences of the occupation cause harm to Iraqi citizens as well as to international peace and security—harm that exceeds Saddam's crimes. There is a paradox in this regard that annuls the credibility of the American claim to be a protector of human rights and rule of law. It is that Saddam Hussein, as a Muslim and Arab, has not been provided a fair trial similar to that of the Nazi leaders who were tried in Nuremberg in the aftermath of the Second World War. It is worth mentioning that Saddam's crimes against his people cannot be equated with the Nazi crimes, nor with the crimes of the American administration and its friends in the pro-Iran Iraqi Shiite political parties. Saddam's trial is unfair and unprofessional because the racist American administration believes that the Muslim and Arab human being does not deserve more.

Several American and Western figures have spoken out about the racist policies practiced by the American administration against the Iraqi people. Some of them clearly and courageously expressed their concerns and denounced the policies of the American administration. They pointed to the trial of Saddam as one of a series of insults that target Muslims and Arabs. Among these is the former American chief justice, Ramsey Clark, who joined the international defense team of Mr. Hussein. This team is known as the Emergency Committee of Iraq. Others that have criticized American policies include the former French foreign minister, the former Malaysian prime minister, Mahateer Mohammed, and the former Algerian president, Ahmed bin Bella. Such figures have good reputations and a history of defending their countries' rights as well as people's rights world-wide. Because they are against the fanatic neoconservatives who currently rule the United States, their efforts will not be successful. Obviously, their endeavor is an attempt to avoid setting a legal precedent that will be followed when whosoever opposes the United States' superpower.

Other Courageous Voices

In many Western countries there are institutions and organizations with courage, fairness, and initiative. However, they are submerged in a West that considers itself a pioneer in advocating democracy. There have been several grassroot organizations that opposed the war on Iraq and its impact. Nonetheless, their activities have not found much coverage by the official media that have been busy covering the adventures of the American right-wing and its dirty war against Iraq, its inhuman violations, and the coverage of Saddam Hussein, a former president and a prisoner of war in his underpants. Following is a website which describes activities of volunteer activists. Their main objective is to follow and expose the American crimes in Iraq. They express the voices of a respected and courageous segment of American and Western society:

www.informationclearinghouse.com

This American voluntary group makes an effort to document all events resulting from the American occupation of Iraq. It is impressive to note the number of the observers, their humble resources, and their delicate documentation of the current situation in Iraq including the trial of Saddam Hussein. By typing "Saddam trial," you will come across hundreds of pages and obtain detailed information on the trial and the way in which the court has been established; in addition there are scores of analyses that discuss the illegitimacy of this trial.

The Hidden Facts in Saddam's Trial: U.S. National Archives' Documents 1964–1994

The United States authority releases from time to time documents on American national security and foreign policy issues through the U.S. National Archives that can be accessed on the Internet by typing the following:

National Security Archives, George Washington University.

This center, which is affiliated to George Washington University, is a non-profit research institution that was established in 1985 to organize and document state documents dealing with national security and foreign affairs. It provides, through the Internet, information on American state policy and American relations with the rest of the world. Documents are shown in an impartial and accurate way. The most provoking and informative documents shown by this center have been those dealing with Iraqi-American relations during Saddam's regime. They are directly related to what takes place in Iraq today, especially those related to Saddam's trial. With respect to the cooperation between the United States and the Iraqi government during the 1980s and the Iran-Iraq War, the National Security Archives reveal an abstract of the hidden facts on Saddam's trial. These documents shed light on the current Iraqi scenario and open files that were meant to be closed so that Saddam's trial would proceed according to what has been planned by Iran and the Iraqi Shiite political parties that try Saddam on behalf of Iran and the American occupation.

Under the title "Shaking Hands with Saddam Hussein," you will find surprising documents and astonishing facts along with Secretary of State Donald Rumsfeld's picture shaking hands with Saddam Hussein. Rumsfeld was accompanied by security and political figures during his visit to Baghdad in 1984. They discussed issues of multi-purpose cooperation. The events that became the main cases against Saddam took place during that era, particularly Halabja and al-Dejail. The Halabja massacre and the al-Dejail operation were episodes of American-Iraqi cooperation. What transformed Donald Rumsfeld, the absent witness, into a judge that tries his former partner? Saddam has been transformed into the most famous prisoner in the world, at the mercy of several tides of American and pro-Iran sectarianists that do not know what to do with him. His destroyed country is in a civil war and will possibly be balkanized. These documents expose the contradictions and double standards that characterize American policy in occupied Iraq.

Who Used Chemical Weapons in Halabja—Saddam or Iran?

The court that tries Mr. Hussein has added another serious case against him; it involves the Kurdish city of Halabja that suffered a painful human tragedy. Halabja was attacked by chemical weapons on March 16, 1988. Hundreds of children, women, and elderly were killed, their bodies scattered in the streets. This massacre is considered the ugliest event in the Iran-Iraq war. Who attacked Halabja with chemical weapons? Why was this tragedy not publicized when it took place? What was the reaction of the American government at the time? Why was Saddam not condemned at that time if the U.S. government thought Saddam had committed this crime? Why did the United States accuse him of this crime later? Fourteen years later, the American president used this incident as one of the justifications for his war against Iraq.

Saddam Hussein is being tried using evidence selected by the American occupation and pro-Iran political parties that are in charge of his trial. The facts on serious cases such as the Halabja massacre are presented only from a single point of view where there are scores of versions, hundreds of documents, and trustworthy witnesses that could help any impartial judge to find the truth about what actually took place during Saddam's regime. The prosecution pursues justice by illuminating specific phases of time while concealing other phases that have unwanted implications. Such is the American-Iranian justice we observe today in Iraq through Saddam's trial.

One of the most significant pieces of information on the Halabja massacre was brought about when the Pentagon assigned the American Defense Intelligence Agency to investigate the case. The Agency visited the scene and collected natural and human samples. They studied and analyzed these samples and produced their report in 1990 and it was published later in the *New York Times*. Professor Stephen Pelletiere, who participated in the report, provided one of the most significant conclusions of the Halabja investigative report. Professor Pelletiere stated that the Iraqi Kurds of Halabja were caught up between Iraqi and Iranian forces at the end of the Iran-Iraq war. In that battle both sides used chemical weapons, however, it was the Iranian gas, not the Iraqi chemicals that killed people in Halabja. He explained that according to the condition of the bodies found, they had been killed by a chemical agent that Iranians had, that Iraqis did not possess. Therefore, Bush's use of the phrase "use poisonous gas against his own people" as a reason to topple Saddam's regime is not supported by the evidence in Halabja.

In an article in the *New York Times* on January 31, 2003 entitled "A War Crime or an Act of War?" Pelletiere wrote, "It was no surprise that President Bush, lacking smoking-gun evidence of Iraq's weapon programs, used his State of the Union address to reemphasize the moral cause for an invasion." In the article he quoted President Bush: "The dictator who is assembling the world's most dangerous weapons has already used them on whole villages, leaving thousands of his own citizens dead, blind, or disfigured."

Stephen Pelletiere, researcher, analyst, and investigator in the C.I.A., played a significant role investigating the Iran-Iraq war as well as the Halabja massacre. He has found no evidence of death resulting from Saddam's chemical weapons. Yet, that is one of the main charges against Saddam Hussein in his trial. Such testimony is evidence of the nonexistent justice in the trial of Saddam Hussein. Professor Pelletiere's testimony and hundreds of statements and documented stories raise clouds of doubt on the real planner and executor of the Halabja massacre. In Saddam's trial, the judges are his historical enemies and the court procedures take place in a primitive way that does not meet the standards of courts in the United States, an alleged defender of human rights. Yet the U.S. is the de facto defender of the trial.

Documentary on Saddam's Trial

Recently, a documentary appeared in France titled "A Story of a Concluded Trial." It was produced by the French producer Jan Pierre and aired by the ATRE Company. It focuses on the ambiguity with which Saddam's trial has been surrounded by the American administration. It contains pictures, documents, and testimony of political figures linked to the trial of Saddam Hussein. It took more a year and a half to prepare the material for this documentary. During this time, the producer traveled to Iraq, Jordan, Spain, and the United States in order to collect testimony and documents related to the trial. The documentary introduces a collection of statements by international law and judiciary experts. It raises many embarrassing questions to the American administration as well as the Shiite political parties under the guidance and blessing of the Iranian *huza*. The producer states that his objective is to unravel the ambiguity of this unprecedented trial. This documentary is an attempt to grasp the motivation and objectives of the figures that administer this trial.

Interference in the Court Process

The Shiite political parties in the Iraqi government began their interference in Saddam's trial through the media by reporting that the Kurdish judge, Rarkaz Amin, was weak and hesitant. This coincided with the assassination by secret Shiite militias of Iraqis who were suspected of disloyalty to the Iraqi government. This put tremendous pressure on the judge, who resigned. The judge complained that the government had pressured him to hasten the court process and issue a verdict. Tensions escalated after the assassination by the militia of two members of Saddam's defense team. These events exposed the American president's lie of "liberation of the Iraqis." The American administration, in fact, replaced Saddam's dictatorship with a theocratic one that has been fraught with daily killing, anarchy, tyranny, and terrorism.

Another example of Iranian interference in the court process was when Iran's deputy foreign minster told the Iranian News Agency in April 2006 that a senior judge would visit Tehran to gather documents on Saddam Hussein. Such a statement exposes the fact that the American occupation of Iraq is nominal while Iran is the de facto occupier of Iraq. Is Iran a neutral party? Will Iran be impartial in evaluating the information submitted to the judge? If the judge was keen to achieve justice, why he did not travel to the United States where he would find factual information and documents, and where witnesses exist whose testimony will accurately describe what took place during Saddam's regime? In such trials, it is improper to gather documents from an adversary. It is also improper to mention Saddam's atrocities against Iran without mentioning Iran's atrocities against Iraq's prisoners of war during the Iran-Iraq war and other crimes committed by both sides.

6

The Iran-American Court Executes Saddam Hussein: The Last Chapter in the Life of a Controversial Figure

The verdict of the Iran-American court in the trial of Saddam Hussein was in harmony with Iraq's current political situation. It has been a situation of rare turmoil in international relations after the American occupation of Iraq resulted in an utter Iranian occupation of that country. The occupational authority has become a mere onlooker with no role and its continuing presence generates a serious danger to regional and international security. The American occupation of Iraq began with no plan and continues without a goal. It continues, presumably, to save the reputation of the American president and his administration so they can avoid admitting the mistake of invading Iraq. The American and Iraqi peoples have to bear the consequences of this adventure, while the only beneficiary is the Islamic Republic regime in Iran. This is, in fact, such a complex issue that it will be dealt with in a separate book.

The present judge, a Kurd who was a political prisoner during Saddam's regime, has issued a verdict of guilty and a sentence of execution. Saddam will remain a controversial figure even after his death because his trial is illegitimate. Experts in law and international relations from all over the world have observed scores of illegalities in the Saddam Hussein trial that will be subjected to future law research. Several barbaric and terrorist acts have accompanied this trial, such as the kidnapping and assassination of two lawyers for the defense. It is known that Iranian intelligence directed these murders. The Iraqi government, dominated by religious political parties associated with Iran, pressured the first judge to the point where he resigned. Also, the Iraqi government remained silent about the terrorism practiced against Saddam's lawyers.

In such a fiasco, the decision to execute Saddam Hussein seems natural. The court process and verdict remind us of the justice system in Iran during the Islamic revolution. These courts executed wounded prisoners of war, musicians, and artists in public places. Mr. Hussein, in cooperation with the United States and others, deterred expansion of the barbaric revolution of the fanatic Khomeini in 1979. It is a paradox that Saddam's court is now controlled by Iran. The authority of the American occupation is responsible for this shameful trial. Regrettably, in the American Iraq, Khomeini's culture, values, and beliefs dominate all aspects of Iraqi society. While calling for democracy and human rights, the occupational authority supports an Iranian-style Iraqi theocracy. Consciously or unconsciously America has accomplished what Iran has been trying to achieve for more than three decades.

Neither circumstance nor time has been conducive to a fair trial for Saddam Hussein. The American occupation has transformed Iraq into an Iranian satellite. Iranian influence takes the form of religious, fascist political oppression. On the other hand, the Kurdish political parties enjoy a nominal participation. Jalal Talabani, the Kurdish president of Iraq, with ceremonial presidential powers, is a friend of Iran and its intelligence agencies. Iran uses Iraq's Kurds as decor for its ideological project in Iraq. The execution of Saddam will enhance the confidence of Iranian leaders and Iraqi Khomeinians in their dark project. Such a project, in fact, transcends Iraq's boundaries through alliances with militant Islamic groups all over the Arab and Islamic world.

Where are America's national interests and security? At the peak of his pride and arrogance, the American president justified his war on Iraq by saying it would avoid the necessity of fighting on American streets. Bush's fearful image could become a reality if the situation in Iraq is not resolved. The execution of Saddam will cause a relapse in the so-called war on terror. If executed, Saddam will become a tool to enhance fundamentalist discourse in the Middle East. Fundamentalist organizations will try to prove that discrimination was practiced against a Muslim and Arab president. They will point out that the trial provided for Saddam was not up to international standards as were trials provided to leaders accused of similar crimes. Saddam's execution will be an example of a double standard for terrorists who target American interests.

Saddam Hussein never sympathized with religious groups; rather, he dealt with both Sunni and Shiite groups harshly. Nonetheless, his execution would trigger the sympathy of religious groups, as he was both Arab and Muslim. Iran, having influence over fundamentalist groups, including Sunni groups, will use Saddam's execution to unleash a divisive battle against American interests all over the world. So far, Islamic organizations have responded with indifference to the news that Saddam will be executed, waiting for it to take place. But it is expected that once Saddam is executed they will charge the United States with the responsibility of executing an Arab Muslim president after giving him an unfair trial. American interests will then provide a divine target for these organizations. In such eventuality, Iran will dominate in the region and the United States will embark upon a long-term war of attrition with the Muslim peoples.

While attempting to export the Iranian revolution to Iraq during the Iran-Iraq war, the Iranian courts executed even children under the age of eighteen in response to their refusal to go to the front. The court that tries Saddam has not been keen to look for the truth regarding the confrontation between the Saddam regime and that of Khomeini, including events at al-Dejail. The verdict on al-Dejail was built on testimony by Saddam's enemies, members of the religious political parties currently in power in Iraq. Historically these enemies had raised arms and planned to assassinate Saddam, enlisting innocent citizens who believed that his assassination would lead them to heaven. Unfortunately, these historical facts, along with details and real witnesses have been absent in this trial. As a result, the world has lost an opportunity to grasp what actually took place during Saddam's regime. As well, a precedent could have been set for similar trials. However, justice has been concealed in the new Khomeini/American era in Iraq. It is an era where destruction, death, and anarchy prevail.

Documents and circumstantial evidence suggest that crimes and atrocities committed by Iranians as well as Americans during four years of occupation have been more severe and ugly than what was committed during Saddam's regime. Saddam's trial by the puppet Iraqi government has violated international law on prisoners of war, and Saddam will be executed by a weak court whose planners have not been successful in concealing its Iranian features. Researchers have a responsibility to reinvestigate this trial and transform it into a historical symbol of the Khomeini/American era. Such reinvestigation, even after Saddam's execution, would create a cautionary tale about the abortion of justice through ideology and selfish interests. The American administration and the British government claim to be guardians of democracy and human rights. The fact that they could be appeased by the verdict reached in Saddam's trial is insupportable. Any future political and lawful scrutiny of Saddam's trial, a process that revived memories of the Iranian Islamic revolutionary courts, should be an embarrassment for them.

Saddam never claimed to be democratic. He was harsh on his enemies, even when they were relatives. One the other hand, his enemies were harsh, too. Important realities of Iraq's history, its effects on the Middle East, and its effects on the rest of the world have been lost because the undeclared America/Iran alliance in Iraq has concealed facts about what took place historically, and what is taking place right now. History, like the new mass graves that have been made by the American/Iranian occupation, is concealed and forgotten.

7

The Execution of Saddam: Justice—America-Iran Style

Saddam Hussein's execution was performed in a way harmonious with the administration of Iraq under the America-Iran occupation. In justifying his invasion of Iraq, the American president emphasized his country's objective to extend democracy to that country and to the Middle East at large. For several reasons the objectives of President Bush and the American neoconservatives have failed. The operation led to a negative outcome—actually, to a total fiasco.

The world has watched as Iraq has been transformed into a huge graveyard, a country out of history under America-Iran control. The American president, after keeping Iraq under total Iranian dominance, modeled the October 2005 trial of Iraq's former president after the paradigm of the infamous Iranian revolutionary courts in the aftermath of the Khomeini revolution of 1979. These actions have destroyed U.S. credibility as a champion of democracy and human rights.

In a small, semi-dark room where some Quranic verses and sectarian emblems in the Iranian style were written on a black banner, Saddam entered handcuffed, accompanied by four masked guards who belong to the ruling Shiite political parties. The world held its breath as Saddam was tied to the gallows. The scene of Saddam's execution has no equivalence but in the Dark Ages; it will stick in mankind's memory, a shock for the world and its conscience. The execution took place in coincidence with a holy Muslim day. It was a twofold message from the Iran-America occupation.

The Shiite government chose to portray its sectarian identity and its separateness from the majority of the Muslim world (Shiites represent 14 percent of 1.2 billion Muslims). Showing no recognition of or respect for one of the most important Muslim holy occasions, they chose to execute Saddam Hussein. The security advisor of the Iraqi government claimed Saddam appeared weak and scared during his execution. Later on, a cell phone video showed that Saddam was composed and calm; he performed his last prayer in unmatched firmness.

Bush's dream of transforming the Middle East, starting with Iraq, has collapsed due to Iraqi resistance. In his failure to face and frustrate the Iranian plan to execute Saddam, President Bush revealed the real Iranian hegemony over Iraq and Iran's capability of frustrating plans of the American administration in the Middle East, particularly in Iraq. By dashing off Saddam's execution, the Iraqi Shiite government wanted to appease a terrorist religious group led by Muqtada al-Sadr whose father had been executed during Saddam's rule. Saddam's head was the required price to stop the fanatic religious leader from creating hurdles for the Iraqi government and supporting unnecessary fighting against the American army.

This was not the first time an Iranian plan met with American acceptance in Iraq. Whatever has been offered by the American people in blood and treasure during the unjustified American presence has been offered to meet the Iranian presence that extends beyond Iran for the first time in 35 years. It is unfortunate that the American people have been misled by the Bush administration about what is and what has been taking place in Iraq. The media seem to be incapable of reflecting the reality in Iraq. Some of the American journalists are intentionally misleading. If Saddam's execution conformed to the rule of law as America declares, why was it performed by disguised officers?

Saddam's execution was preceded by some suspicious activities by elements of the Iranian intelligence in Iraq. The American army in Baghdad captured some of them. Apparently they were caught by accident because the Iranian presence now is far beyond sending a few individuals for a specific task. The Shiite Iraqi rulers and Iran's intelligence are skillful in utilizing the formidable American forces in Iraq. The American and world media paid much attention to the Iranian officials' arrest in Baghdad. Some considered it a late American attempt to correct the situation and dismantle the clandestine Iranian state in Iraq. But the suspects were released after the pro-Iran Shiite Iraqi government made contacts with American officials. These contacts were made hours before Saddam's execution.

Rumors have circulated that Saddam was assassinated by pro-Iran militia. The Iraqi government has confessed that militia members, through the blessing of one of the influential Shiites, sneaked into the execution chamber and performed Saddam's execution. Saddam's execution was the legal and moral responsibility of both the American administration and Iran in addition to the Shiite political partics that constitute the Iraqi government. Such a drama makes the United States government look like a tool used by a fascist government and professional killers.

Saddam's assassination led to condemnation of the United States that will persist regardless of the dubious excuses made by the American government. Saddam's assassination is a reflection of the current Iraq in which barbarism and fascism prevail. In today's Iraq, kidnapping, secret prisons, mass graveyards, killing, and other crimes far exceed what has been attributed to Saddam Hussein's crimes against humanity.

In December 2006 Saddam's lawyers presented a memorandum of three hundred pages appealing the execution verdict. The higher court, consisting mostly of religious political parties that had been in Iran during Saddam's regime, took three weeks to reject the appeal. Some legal experts mentioned that to process such an appeal might take three years under a system that respects the rule of law.

Major and Minor Players in Saddam's Execution

The first player is the American president George W. Bush. He could have delayed Saddam's execution but he is in a weak position. He chose to be silent and cooperate with the Shiite government as he understands its ties with Iran. The Iraqi government, with its close ties to Iran, will not cease blackmailing President Bush who has been unable to manage Iraq's situation in a way that preserves his country's interests. To avoid disclosing his role in misleading the American people until he finds a solution to the Iraqi fix, Bush must cooperate with the transitional Iraqi government. The coming days will reveal the personal dilemma of President Bush in Iraq and his weakness in dealing with the Shiite Iraqi government.

The second player is Khalil Zada, the American ambassador to Iraq. Calling him ambassador is deceiving for his duties have nothing to do with diplomacy. He is a security and military coordinator between his government and the Iraqi government. Before Saddam's execution, Zada participated in negotiations between Shiite Iraqis, who are ideologically and politically tied to Iran, and inexperienced American army officers in charge of guarding Saddam. The Iraqi faction achieved it goals of executing Saddam as Iran and the Shiite circles had planned.

Participation in Saddam's execution has involved individuals trained ideologically, politically, and militarily in Iran, such as Nouri al-Maliki, the current prime minister, Muafaq al-Rabia'i, a security councilor who declared his government's approval of the execution, and Abdul Aziz al-Hakim, Iran's number one man in Iraq and chairman of the Supreme Council of the Islamic Revolution in Iraq.

Political Consequences of Saddam's Execution

Saddam's execution will enhance the postoccupation problems in Iraq. It will also enhance Iranian hegemony over Iraq and increase the risk of strategic imbalance in the Middle East. It is considered a sacred victory for fanatics in Iran as well as Iraq. It will increase hatred for the United States in the Muslim world and will enhance the discourse of violent groups, imparting them unprecedented credibility. In the United States it is anticipated that American people will come to realize the magnitude of Iranian dominance in Iraq. The American administration is torn between the Iraqi resistance that is supported by the Iraqi people, and the Iranian hegemony over Iraq that seeks to blackmail the American president and compel him to make deals.

The execution of Saddam was a holy victory for the extremist Shiites in Iran and Iraq. The American president went on an unusual trip to Iraq for four years; he did not return until today. In the same time the holy Iranian leader Ayatollah Khomeini emerged from his grave and sat on his chair at the White House, dominating the mind and actions of the president who uses the blood and money of his country to implement the wishes of the Iranian leader. This fantasy turned into reality for millions of ordinary Shiites in Iran and Iraq who believe that their holy leader controlled the mind of the American president.

President Bush completed his mission in Iraq. The result is a theocratic state, loyal to Iran and the Bush administration, where war crimes and genocide are committed by the government. The American president suffers a case of political schizophrenia, rare in the history of international relations. He is engaged in Iranian strategy and claims he is against Iran. Iraq is host to the second hidden holocaust in the history of the mankind; this will be the subject of my next book on Iraq.

8

Iraq after Freedom

Over 3000 American soldiers have died in order that the Bush administration might establish an Islamic theocracy in the formerly secular Iraq. Now sectarian violence has made Iraq the most dangerous place in the world as civil war rages.

Under the regime of Saddam Hussein, Christians had been allowed to peacefully conduct their business without fear. Under U.S. and British liberation, many Christians are closing their shops. Also, church officials have been attacked. His Grace, Bishop Mar Adai of the Assyrian Church of the East was attacked on the streets of Baghdad. His assailants wanted to steal the gold cross from around his neck.

The Iraqi Minority: The Suffering of Iraqi Christian People Today

Christian people in Iraq are being exposed to all kinds of persecution every day. As a minority with no backing, they are an easy target. They are tormented and crushed in a jungle-like world where survival of the fittest rules. I'm writing today about this painful and bitter situation to tell people all over the world about the reality of daily life for Christians in Iraq.

For the last three years life in Iraq has been very difficult. Peace and stability are deteriorating day by day as armed militants roam the streets. Some examples are:

(1) Unjustified killing and assassination of highly educated people (professors, doctors, businessmen, and high ranking officers in the army) is common. Many innocent people are being crushed in this so-called new democratic era.

(2) Car bombs and road bombs are killing people every day under the pretext of resistance. Who is resisting whom? Or what?

(3) Terrorists are kidnapping and killing liquor store owners just because they are Christians. The terrorists claim that selling and drinking alcohol in Iraq is forbidden. According to what law? It is the law of the jungle. Terrorists send threatening letters to Christian families demanding ransoms, demanding they close of

their stores or leave their houses or convert to Islam. Otherwise, the terrorists threaten, the stores will be bombed, the children will be kidnapped, and the houses will be destroyed.

(4) The Iraqi people who work with the Americans are considered traitors, especially the Christians who are put in the same category as the British and Americans because they share the same religion.

This was part of an evil plan designed by Muslims who infiltrated the country to deprive the original Christian Iraqi nation of its patriotic identity; to deny it belonged to Iraq and to treat Christians as second class citizens. Casualties are high. One family may lose several members. Christian women and girls are forced to cover their heads and wear long dresses in schools and universities. Christian children are forced to attend Islamic lessons in school and history lessons are filled with Islamic teachings.

Facts Denied by the Bush Administration

Shiite parties with religious and ideological Iranian foundations control the Iraqi state and coordinate with Iran in all affairs of the country, especially in Iraqi army and security forces. Iran can expel the American army from Iraq at any time with the cooperation of the Iraqi government. The secret alliance between the American administration and Shiite political and army forces weakens the occupation army; this will lead to the establishment of a confederation state consisting of Iraq and Iran.

Iran is now a real threat to world peace and security. American polices in Iraq made that possible. It is impossible to reduce the danger of Iran with military force because that would lead to destruction of regional and international peace. This would result in collapse of the world economy and the spread of anarchy and terrorism. How to end or minimize the Iranian threat to the world?

It is difficult to see a resolution of the conflict in Iraq with the current American administration policy. The Bush administration tried to appease the extremist Shiites who govern Iraq and participated in violation of international laws by allowing prisoners of war to face illegal trials similar to the notorious Iranian Islamic revolutionary courts. The American administration did not gain anything from cooperating with the Iraqi Shiite government loyal to Iran. To return Iraq to its pre-Saddam situation is impossible; the conflict between Sunni and Shiite that remained latent for so many years has been inflamed to a point where communication between the two factions has been destroyed. America must bear the legal and ethical responsibility for the current chaotic situation and the genocide sponsored by Iran and the Iraqi Shiite militia which controls military and security forces.

The Kurdish political bloc in Iraq is very weak; the Kurdish president Jalal Talabani is without power. In addition, Talabani is one of the oldest Iranian agents in Iraq. Repair and modification of this abnormal and dangerous situation will be difficult because Iran possesses the keys to Iraqi security and politics. In fact, the American authority in Iraq is exposed to great deception by Iranian intelligence and by the Shiite government.

The Bush administration has tried to hide these facts, but eventually the world will know the details of events in Iraq from the first day of the American invasion. This will be a strong blow to the image of the American state.

Who Made the Decision?

Who made the decision to execute the former Iraqi president? All evidence says the decision was issued before the Iraqi court gave the verdict, by agents of the Iranian theocratic "court."

Prior to the Execution

Before his execution, Saddam composed a letter to the Iraqi people calling on them to continue fighting against the occupiers, to expel invaders from Iraq, but to not hate the people belonging to the invading countries. G. W. Bush asked not to be wakened when Saddam was executed. This is nothing new—the same president slept for four years while Iraq gradually entered the dark ages, until it slipped under the control of the Iranian Islamic state. President Bush finally awakened when Iraq had become an Iranian province.

Saddam's defense team tried to force the American administration to assume responsibility for protecting the former Iraqi president under international law and the Geneva convention. But the Bush administration failed to stop the execution of Saddam by the Iranian-Iraqi sectarian court. The American president avoided conflict with the government of Iraq because he did not want to draw the attention of the American people to the political results of the war on Iraq and the grave situation in Iraq that has resulted from his policies.

The Bush administration handed over the prisoner of war Saddam Hussein to the militias of the Iraqi government loyal to Iran. The former Iraqi president spent the last days of his life in a small cell, depending on the occupation authority and his lawyer. Saddam met two of his relatives who said Saddam was looking like a person on his way to his wedding night, not a prisoner on his way to death. The relatives cried when Saddam told them about his holy Quran book which had been with him throughout four years of imprisonment. Saddam called the holy book "the comrade who does not cheat or lie." The story of Saddam Hussein from his arrest until his assassination is being written by Saddam's lawyer; it is expected the book will contain many secrets and several documents handwritten by the former Iraqi president.

Saddam Hussein, who ruled Iraq for more than 35 years, found himself surrounded by a historical enemy—the masked extremist Shiite, who failed to defeat him for 35 years but finally succeeded through the agency of G. W. Bush. On his way to the death chamber, the former Iraqi president saw his beloved city Baghdad for the last time through a narrow hole in the American armored vehicle which transferred him to the execution site. The strong leader walked the last steps of his life accompanied by a masked Shiite. A few hours prior to the execution of Saddam Hussein, the Iraqi prime minister Nouri al-Maliki contacted his leader the Iranian extremist Ali al-Sistani who decreed that Saddam would be killed on the holy Muslim day Eid. The government of Iraq deliberately ordered the execution of Saddam on a Muslim holy day to create sympathy with the resistance. Saddam marched in steady steps toward the bench of penalty; Iraqi television cameras broadcast part of the penalty but removed important snapshots that showed the rare courage of the former Iraqi president. Iraqi security adviser Muwaffoq Rubaie claimed falsely that Saddam was shaken and fragile during the penalty. The whole world knows he was lying after viewing footage of the execution photographed by a mobile phone. Saddam was more than strong—he scoffed at the Shiite and Iranian agents who attended the penalty. Saddam ended on the gallows; his body was transferred by a member of the Shiite militia in an ambulance where jokes were made about the corpse.

The Iraqi tragedy has not ended with Saddam; what happened was compatible with the Shiite political culture of Iranian origin which emerged after the Khomeini revolution in Iran in 1979. Strange indeed is the role of the United States of America, a state that claims to be at war with terrorism, and especially with the Iranian model of government. President Bush used the influence and power of the United States to prepare a barbaric Iranian model of penalty and then to administer it.

A few days before the American invasion of Iraq, the American president stood alone against the international community. He violated international law again prior to the execution of the former Iraqi president. The U.S. president repeated the same old position and stood against the majority of free world governments and organizations. But to participate in the killing of Saddam Hussein, president G. W. Bush was forced to stand with the Iranian-Iraqi alliance who rule

Iraq. President Bush calls the Iraqi government a democratic government and describes himself as a liberation hero, but is this the truth? History will answer this question. The American people who elected this president don't know the truth. They expect their country to support the values of freedom, justice, and democracy. But their president was forced by the Iranian-Iraqi alliance to take another direction. Violation of international laws and violation of the American constitution—these are crimes that will not soon be forgotten.

After the Execution of Saddam: Bush with Iran and Against the World

The way the execution of Saddam Hussein was allowed to take place shows the ethical weakness of the American administration and demonstrates that it does not care about international laws and norms.

Most world governments and organizations condemned in strong terms the execution of Saddam Hussein. States that supported the execution of the former Iraqi president were those that participated in the occupation of Iraq—the United States of America, Australia, and England. In Iran, the historical and ideological enemy of Saddam Hussein, there was huge joy among leaders (ayatollahs) of the theocratic regime. They went in batches to the grave of the Iranian holy leader Ayatollah Khomeini to celebrate the execution of Saddam Hussein, a divine victory bestowed on them by the American president. After the killing of Saddam, the Iraqi Shiite government loyal to Iran will act independently of the American administration and the occupation authority because it doesn't need them any more. The hidden Islamic state of Iraq that will very soon be a copy of the Iranian regime has been established with the cooperation of the American administration who built the theoretical and practical basis of this state.

The Iraqi government has continued to implement methods of the famous Iranian Islamic revolutionary court. It has executed two aides of Saddam Hussein and, according to a medical report from inside Iraq, has massacred a half brother of Saddam. The American administration will be responsible historically for the adoption of barbaric behavior by the Iranian government of Iraq. This ideological behavior continues in Iraq: crimes against humanity, secret prisons, the killing and torture of opponents. These crimes are documented and impossible to hide or deny. The Bush administration is unable to control the situation because it is still caught up in the lies it told before the invasion of Iraq, during the occupation of Iraq, and after the transition of power to the Iraqi government. The present Iraqi government consists of Iranian terrorist organizations bearing the name of political parties.

The Bush administration continues to lie. President Bush warns every day of the consequences of failure in Iraq; he says that the failure in Iraq is a victory for terrorism. By terror he means al-Qaeda. But this organization has no grassroots in any of the Muslim countries; thus there is no need to invade the world's countries, and no need to spend billions of dollars and kill hundred of thousands of innocent people to defeat and eliminate this organization. Al-Qaeda and other religious extremist organizations—Sunni or Shiite—were unable to work in Saddam's Iraq for more than 25 years. But al-Qaeda and other extremist organizations have infiltrated Iraq as a result of the American invasion. However, the biggest danger is not al-Qaeda which has a very small group of people in Iraq; the bigger danger is state-terrorism—specifically the Iranian state which completely controls Iraq. The American president is dishonest with his people and the world by continuing to exaggerate the danger from terrorism organizations in Iraq. To conceal the fact that Iraq is under the control of Iran, the American administration continues the deception that the current Iraqi government is different from the theocratic regime of Iran. Actually, separation between these two regimes is impossible because the relations between them are based on life or death for both of them. Do the American people know the horrific facts about post-Saddam Iraq which indirectly supports Iran's nuclear project? Post-Saddam Iraq will become a storehouse of nuclear reactors for Iran.

The new Iraq, established by the Bush administration, is on a dangerous path. Attempts to deal with the current situation in Iraq by the American administration are doomed to failure. The Bush administration must now choose between its reputation and regional and global security—one must be sacrificed to keep the other.

The International Committee for the Defense of former President Saddam Hussein

Not far from the court room where Saddam Hussein was being tried for crimes against humanity, the Shiite militia, which controls the Iraqi army and police was monitoring events in the court. During the trial, two of Saddam's defense team were kidnapped from their offices by the Iranian-Iraqi organization known as Badr—the military wing of the supreme council of the Islamic revolution in Iraq. This council is trained and funded by Iran and controls the government of Iraq which is supported by the American administration. Ten masked men wearing Iraqi police uniforms and carrying guns kidnapped two of Saddam's lawyers and tortured them to death. These masked groups have become the common denominator in the American-Iranian justice system in the new Iraq.

The sentence to execute Saddam Hussein was issued by a secret court prior to the mock-trial of Saddam. The secret court was headed by the spiritual leader of Iraqi Shiites, the Iranian citizen Ali al-Sistani, the real ruler of Iraq after the American liberation and democracy. Ramsey Clark—lawyer and activist, formerly with the U.S. Department of Justice—and Mahathir Mohamad, a former prime minister of Malaysia, made serious attempts to try Saddam Hussein within the framework of the law. But the trial of the former Iraqi president was a formality, its mission being only to recite the decision that had been made previously by the secret court, the decision to execute Saddam Hussein. Several hours before the execution of Saddam, the Iraqi prime minister, the executive chairman of the secret government of Iraq, telephoned the Khomeini of American Iraq, Ali al-Sistani, to determine if it would be possible to execute Saddam Hussein on the day of the Islamic holiday Eid.

Thanks to the American administration and president Bush, Iraq has returned to the dark ages. The urbanization of modern Iraq was executed along with Saddam. What a shame. In an era of terrorism, the East and the West finally met under the banner of the sectarian court trying Saddam Hussein. The court was illegal from beginning to end; U.S. attorney Ramsey Clark used his legal and political experience to argue for the former Iraqi president but the judge, who recently escaped from Iraq after his cheap role in the assassination of Saddam, followed the instructions of the Iraqi sectarian government and Iran. The judge implemented the instructions of the occupation authority and Iran in spite of Ramsey Clark who took a courageous position inside the sectarian court. The global media delivered strong words of condemnation by Mahathir Mohamad who compared the execution of Saddam to a lynching in the manner of an ugly period in the history of the United States—when slaves were hanged from trees. The United States of America, like Iraq, returned to the dark ages.

Mahathir Mohamed is a moderate Islamic thinker and peaceful person, one who rejects the use of religion in politics. Here he comments on the trial and execution of Saddam Hussein:

> The world watched in horror at the barbaric lynching of the former president of Iraq, Saddam Hussein, allegedly for crimes against humanity. This public murder was sanctioned by the war criminals, U.S. President George W. Bush and British Prime Minister Tony Blair. The trial was a mockery of justice, no more than a kangaroo court. Defense counsels were brutally murdered; witnesses were threatened; judges were removed for being impartial, then replaced by puppet judges. Yet, we are told that Iraq was invaded to promote democracy, freedom, and justice.

A peaceful country has been turned into a war zone. Over 500,000 children died as a result of criminal economic sanctions, and the latest findings by the medical journal Lancet reveals that over 650,000 Iraqis have died since the illegal invasion in 2003. The war criminal Bush has killed more Iraqis than President Saddam, if in fact Saddam was guilty of any crime. If President Saddam Hussein is guilty of war crimes, then the world must find Bush and Blair equally guilty and the International Criminal Court cannot but prosecute these war criminals. The inaction thus far by the International Criminal Court against Bush and Blair exposes the double standard of the said Court, when it does not hesitate to prosecute war crimes committed in Darfur, Rwanda, and Kosovo.

If we support human rights and justice, we must condemn this barbaric lynching of former president Saddam Hussein. There can be no excuse whatsoever for this injustice. War criminal Bush and the puppet regime in Iraq have made a mockery of the rule of law.

Dr. Mahathir Mohamad
Former prime minister of Malaysia

In another statement, Mahathir Mohamed reiterates:

As a member of the International Committee set up to oversee the trial of Saddam Hussein, I would like to express my horror and disgust over the trial and sentencing of Saddam Hussein to death by hanging.

First, a court comprised of his enemies has no right to try Saddam Hussein. Since the inception of the trial, the International Committee and the panel of lawyers for the defense of Saddam Hussein have repeatedly pointed out that a court set up by an illegal occupying power has no jurisdiction whatsoever to conduct the said proceedings. If Saddam Hussein is to be tried, it should be by an international court of judges drawn from countries uninvolved in the Iraqi invasion and occupation. The members of the International Committee have demanded that in order for justice to be done and seen to be done, the trial court and the judges must be independent and without bias, and be able to discharge their duties without fear or favor. The chief judge presiding in the early part of the proceedings resigned in protest against blatant interference by the Iraqi regime installed by the occupying power. He was replaced by a judge who had no qualms in disregarding all established principles of fair trial, who was willing to hand down a judgement inconsistent with the evidence adduced.

In the course of the proceedings, lawyers representing Saddam Hussein and his coaccused were threatened and brutally murdered. Witnesses were also intimidated. This fact alone would render any verdict handed down by the court to be manifestly unjust and contrary to all established principles of a fair trial.

There was no evidence that Saddam Hussein was involved in the killings of Shiites in 1982. Yet the court found him guilty. This was a kangaroo court set up for the sole purpose of rendering a guilty verdict. It was a Nuremberg type court, manifestly biased and incapable of being just.

If Saddam Hussein was guilty as charged, then President George W. Bush and Prime Minister Tony Blair should be tried for the unlawful invasion and occupation of Iraq and the death of over 650,000 Iraqis and the brutal torture of thousands of innocent men, women, and children in Abu Ghraib and Guantanamo Bay.

President Bush Senior, President Clinton, and President Bush Junior should also be tried for sanctions against Iraq which caused the deaths of more than half-a-million children and the use of illegal weapons such as depleted uranium, cluster bombs, and phosphorus bombs.

For all these reasons, as a member of the International Committee overseeing the trial of Saddam Hussein, I condemn the death sentence passed on Saddam Hussein. It is a travesty of justice and unworthy of the present stage of human civilization.

Dr. Mahathir Mohamad
Former Prime Minister of Malaysia
Novermber 7, 2006

Before the Big Explosion: What then?

The invasion and occupation of Iraq caused political conflict within the United States of America. The president and his group of neoconservatives hide behind a vague occupation policy to avoid admitting the reality of the disastrous political results of the invasion. These results comprise the full control of Iraq by Iran. G. W. Bush lied to the world and to the American nation. Opponents of Bush administration policies in Iraq in the American congress and the senate talk about pulling out of Iraq without taking responsibility for legal or ethical ramifications. In Iraq there is genocide—more than a half million persons have lost their lives—there are war crimes, unprecedented since the end of World War II. Attempts to hide these facts are eroding the reputation of the United States of America. There is now global protest against the policies of President Bush; this protest will shift to the American state if it does not bear responsibility for the outcome of the situation in Iraq. A possible solution would be to transfer the authority in Iraq from the American administration and the Iraqi government loyal to Iran to an international body for a transitional period. Protection under the auspices of the United Nations and other international organizations would save the lives of millions of Iraqi people and stop the genocide in Iraq. This solution would require recognition of the deadly mistakes of the American president. Urgent action is needed from the international community and the American people to support an international protection plan for the people of Iraq.

Related Links and Resources

I draw the attention of readers to some of the sites and links that contain harrowing scenes of genocide, murder, and torture against hundreds of thousands of innocent Iraqi civilians. Many face death in secret prisons run by death squads sponsored by the theocratic regime of Iran and the Iraqi government, with full protection and support from the American forces in Iraq.

http://www.the fourreasons.org/victimsofwar.htm

http://www.robert-fisk.com/iraqwarvictims_mar2003.htm

http://www.antiwar.com

http://www.gwu.edu/~nsarchivr

http://www.the7thfire.com/Iraq_War/us_war_crimes_in_iraq.htm

http://www.albasrah.net

http://www.informationclearinghouse.com

http://www.brucegourley.com/iraqtheocracy

http://www.iraqirabita.org

http://www.marchforjustice.com/Falluja22.swf

http://www.iraqbodycount.org/background.php

http://www.albasrah.net/images/war_crimes/index.htm

978-0-595-43649-1
0-595-43649-8

Printed in the United States
77070LV00003B/376-393

9 780595 436491